und Andere, Henri Marx

New Music Album for the Piano

und Andere, Henri Marx

New Music Album for the Piano

ISBN/EAN: 9783744792998

Printed in Europe, USA, Canada, Australia, Japan

Cover: Foto ©Thomas Meinert / pixelio.de

More available books at **www.hansebooks.com**

NEW MUSIC ALBUM

FOR THE PIANO.

INDEX.

No.	PAGE.			
1	1	TURLURETTE,	(Quadrille)	H. Marx
2	7	PRAISE OF TEARS,	(Song)	F. Schubert
3	9	CAPTAIN JINKS,	(Song)	T. Maclagan
4	12	VAILLANCE,	(Polka Militaire)	J. Ascher
5	16	ROBINSON CRUSOE.	(Quadrille)	Offenbach
6	21	NOT FOR JOSEPH,	(Song)	Arthur Lloyd
7	24	THE LOVER AND THE BIRD,	(Song)	P. D. Guglielmo
8	27	ORPHEE AUX ENFERS,	(Quadrille)	Offenbach
9	32	JERUSALEM THE GOLDEN,	(Hymn)	A. Ewing
10	33	THE MERRIEST GIRL THAT'S OUT,	(Song)	Arranged by C. Minasi
11	36	COUSIN ET COUSINE,	(Schottisch Elegante)	J. Egghard
12	40	HOW FAIR ART THOU,	(Song)	H. Weidt
13	42	IN THE STARLIGHT,	(Duet) Vocal,	S. Glover
14	46	ON THE BEACH AT CAPE MAY,	(Song)	Words by E. N. Slocum
15	49	SCHÜTZEN-MARSCH,		Carl Faust
16	52	VOLL HUMOR,	(Polka)	Carl Faust
17	55	OHNE ZÜGEL UND BÜGEL,	(Galop)	Carl Faust
18	58	GOOD BYE, SWEETHEART, GOOD BYE,	(Song)	J. L. Hatton
19	61	LA CHATELAINE,	(Polka Mazourka)	Carl Faust
20	64	THE YOUNG RECRUIT,	(March)	B. Richards
21	69	FIVE O'CLOCK IN THE MORNING,	(Ballad)	By Claribel
22	72	THE MOON BEHIND THE TREES,	(Song)	G. T. Wilson
23	75	UP AND DOWN,	(Galop)	Carl Faust
24	79	THE BLACK-KEY,	(Polka Mazurka)	A. Herzog
25	82	ROMANCE FROM DON PASQUALE,*	(Opera Song)	Donizetti
26	86	CRISPINO E LA COMARE,	(Opera Bouffe)	Fantaisie Arranged by E. Ketterer
27	91	HOME SWEET HOME,	(Variation)	J. H. Slack
28	97	MARCHE DES TAMBOURS,	(Militaire)	Sydney Smith
29	103	LES VARIETES PARISIENNES,	(New Quadrille)	
30	108	LA BELLE HELENE	(Galop)	Arranged by D. Godfrey
31	113	COME BACK TO ERIN,	(Song)	Claribel
32	117	ADRIENNE,	(Polka Mazourka)	A. Talexy
33	120	MAGGIE'S SECRET, (My Heart is over the Sea,)	(Song)	Claribel
34	123	IM STRUDEL,	(Galop)	Carl Faust
35	127	BLUE BIRD,	(Polka Redowa)	Weingarten
36	130	BARBE BLEUE,	(Galop)	Arranged by T. A'Becket, Jr.
37	133	THE NAIAD'S,	(Barcarolle)	E. Mack
38	138	FIRE AND FLAME,	(Galop)	Carl Faust
39	141	VICTORIA LANCERS,	(Quadrilles)	Weingarten
40	146	LUCREZIA BORGIA, (Il Brindisi)	(Song)	Donizetti
41	152	SCENES THAT ARE BRIGHTEST, (Maritana)	(Song)	W. V. Wallace
42	154	MY FIRST WIFE'S DEAD, (Barbe Bleue,)	(Song)	Offenbach
43	159	LES ADIEUX,	(Nocturne)	P. Horro
44	162	FRA DIAVOLO,	(Fantaisie)	Arranged by Sidney Smith
45	169	VALSE DES ROSES,	(Waltz)	E. Ketterer
46	175	CUJUS ANIMAM,	(Opera Stabat Mater)	W. Kuhe
47	181	LA FAVORITE,	(Morceau De Concert)	J. Ascher
48	186	IMMORTELLEN,	(Waltz, 4 Hands)	J. Gung'l
49	194	KUNSTLER LEBEN,	(Waltz)	Strauss
50	198	SANGER'S,	(March)	

** Used by permission of Oliver Ditson & Co.*

JULES BERR,

Editor and Publisher,

430 WALNUT STREET,

PHILADELPHIA.

Wm. Ruller & Co., Bookbinders. Samuel Loag, Printer.

Dedicated to Mrs. Luther W. Frost, of Yonkers, N. Y

TURLURETTE
QUADRILLE

POUR

PIANO

Par

HENRI MARX

PUBLISHED BY JULES BERR,

No. 430 Walnut Street,

PHILADELPHIA.

TURLURETTE.

QUADRILLE.

Motifs de VICTOR CHERI. Par H. MARX.

No. 1.
PANTALON.
CODA.
FIN.
TRIO.

 Jules Berr, Publisher.

No. 2.
ÉTÉ.
FIN.
D. C.
2me et 4me Fois.
mf
tr
f
D.C

No. 3.
POULE.

mf
CODA.
sf
1.
al CODA.
p
f

Jules Betz, Publisher.

TURLURETTE.

No. 4. PASTOURELLE.

f
f
mf
p
D.C.

Published by Jules Berr.

No. 5.
FINALE

pp
ff
FINE
1re et 3me Fois.
D.C.
2me et 4me Fois.
D.C.

Flowerets Blooming, Winds Perfuming.

(PRAISE OF TEARS.)

F. SCHUBERT.

Moderato.
8va
PIANO.
pp
1. Flow'rets blooming, winds per - fum-ing, Ev'-ry joy of youth and
2. When the streaming eyes are beaming Thro' the mist of sor - row's
3. Deep grief tell-ing, tears were well-ing, Till they flow'd throughout the
8va.
spring. Soft ca - ress-es beau-ty press-es On the lips that fond - ly
tear, There's a heal-ing Pow'r re - veal-ing Heav'n-ly glimp-ses bright and
world; They sur - round it, and a - round it With their pity-ing arms have

Published by Jules Berr.

cling; Wine-cups flow - ing, nec - tar glow - ing, Mer - ry
clear. Oh, how fleet - ly, calm'd thus sweet - ly, Each wild
curl'd; Earth's dust spurn - ing, art thou yearn - ing For a
dance and fro - lic arts, All the pas-sions' wild-est fash-ions, Can they
thought to rest is hush'd, As the flow-ers, cool'd by show-ers, Lift their
state all free from sin? Then in weep-ing thy soul steep-ing, Let it
ev - er fill our hearts? Can they ev - er fill our hearts?
heads that erst were crush'd, Lift their heads that erst were crush'd.
plunge that flood with - in, Let it plunge that flood with - in.
fp
pp
8va

CAPTAIN JINKS.

T. MACLAGAN.

Allegretto.
PIANO.
1. I am Cap - tain Jinks of the
Horse Marines, I of - ten live be - yond my means, I sport young la - dies
in their teens, To cut a swell in the ar - my. I teach the la - dies how to dance,

Published by Jules Berr.

how to dance, how to dance, I teach the la - dies how to dance, For
Spoken: Ha! ah! ah! CHORUS.
I'm their pet in the ar - my. I'm Cap - tain Jinks of the Horse Marines, I
colla voce.
give my horse good corn and beans; Of course it's quite be - yond my means, Tho' a
cap - tain in the ar - my.
f
Drum.

Published by Jules Berr.

After 1st, 2d & 3d Verses.
After last Verse.

2.

I joined my corps when twenty-one,
Of course I thought it capital fun;
When the enemy came then off I run,
I wasn't cut out for the army.
When I left home, mamma she cried,
Mamma she cried, mamma she cried,
When I left home, mamma she cried,
"He ain't cut out for the army."

Spoken: No, she thought I was too young, but then, I said, ah! mamma,

Chorus.—I'm Captain Jinks, &c.

3.

The first day I went out to drill,
The bugle sound made me quite ill,
At the Balance step my hat it fell,
And that wouldn't do for the army.
The officers they all did shout,
They all cried out, they all did shout,
The officers they all did shout,
"Oh, that's the curse of the army."

Spoken: Of course my hat *did* fall off, but, ah! nevertheless,

Chorus.—I'm Captain Jinks, &c.

4.

My tailor's bills came in so fast,
Forced me one day to leave at last,
And ladies too no more did cast
Sheep's-eyes at me in the army.
My creditors at me did shout,
At me did shout, at me did shout,
My creditors at me did shout,
"Why, kick him out of the army."

Spoken: I said, ah! gentlemen, kick *me* out of the army? Perhaps you are not aware that

Chorus.—I'm Captain Jinks, &c.

VAILLANCE.

POLKA MILITAIRE.

JOSEPH ASCHER.

mf
sf
f
dim.
p
Giocosamente.
Marcato.

p
Sonore.
ff
Ped.
Scherzando.
mf
p
ff
Ben marcato.
mf
ff
Ped.
mf
ff
molto.
dimi - - - - -
Ped.

nuendo.
pp
sempre.
p
f
Sonore.
Scherzando.
mf
p
ff
Ben marcato.
mf
mf
ff
ff
Ped.
*
Ped.
*

Molto-
dimi -
nuendo.
pp
sempre.
p
Marcato.
sf
f
ff
Con
tutta
forza.
8va.
Fine.

Published by Jules Berr.

Robinson Crusoe.

QUADRILLE.

Opéra Comique de J. OFFENBACH.

MUSIC OF THE DANCE. ARBAN.

Pantalon.
1.
mf
f
p
ff
CODA.
TRIO.
Fine.
p
D.C.

8va
2.
ff
8va
mf
tr
p
tr
cres.
f
D.C.

Published by JULES BERR.

Poule.
3.
mf
lourdement.
f
CODA.
ff
TRIO.
sf
p
D.C.

Pastourelle.
8va
4.
ff
8va
ff
p
sf
p
ff
D.C.

Published by Jules Berr.

5.
Finale.

legg.
p
f
ff
(1st and 3d time.)
cres.
(2d and 4th time.)

NOT FOR JOSEPH.

ARTHUR LLOYD.

PIANO.
f
ff
2. I

Published by JULES BERR.

1. Jo - seph Bax - ter is my name, My friends all call me Joe; I'm
used to throw my cash a - bout In a reck - less sort of way; I'm
up, you know, to ev' - ry game, And ev' - ry - thing I know; Ah, I
care - ful now what I'm a - bout, And cau - tious how I pay; Now, the
once was green as green could be; I suf - fer'd for it, though; Now,
oth - er night I ask'd a pal With me to have a drain,— "Thanks,
if they try it on with me, I tell them, not for Joe.
Joe," said he: "let's see, old pal: I think I'll have Champagne." Will ye? said I: oh no,—
p

'Not for Joe,' 'Not for Joe,' If he knows it, Not for Jo-seph; No, no, no, 'Not for Joe,'
'Not for Jo-seph, oh, dear, no.'
f
ff

3.

There's a fellow called Jack Bannister,
He's a sort of chap, is Jack,
Who is always money borrowing
And never pays ye back;
Now, last Thursday night he came to me,
Said he'd just returned to town,
And was rather short of cash,—
Could I lend him half a crown?

Well, said I, if I thought I should get it back again, I would, with pleasure; but excuse me, if I say,—

'Not for Joe,' &c.

4.

A friend of mine, down in Pall Mall,
The other night said, "Joe,
I'll introduce you to a gal
You really ought to know;
She's a widow you should try and win,
'Twould a good match be for you,—
She's pretty, and got lots of tin,
And only forty-two."

Fancy forty-two!—old enough to be my grandmother,—and you know a fella' can't marry his grandmother,—lots of tin, though, and pretty, forty-two! No,

'Not for Joe,' &c.

5.

I think you've had enough of Joe,
And go I really must;
I thank you for your kindness, though,
And only hope and trust
That the favor you have shown so long
I always may retain;
Perhaps now, if you like my song,
You'll wish I'll sing again.

But

'Not for Joe,' &c.

Published by JULES BERR.

The Lover and the Bird.

P. D. GUGLIELMO.

Allegretto non troppo.
PIANO.
p
ad lib.
ppp
8va.
tr
a tempo.
dolcissimo.
1. Oh, sing, sing on sweet-ly to cheer me, Bird, thy mu - sic so-lace will bring,
2. Oh, sing, sing on e'en to de-ceive me, Bird, with vi - sions glitt'ring and vain,
rall.
legato.

 Published by Jules Bory.

Thou wilt not fly: why shouldst thou fear me? Sing of love, of
Vain flatt'ring hopes, oh, do not leave me. Sing of love, of
love on - ly sing. Those ho-ney'd notes of thine thro' me are thrill - ing, This
love on - ly sing. Soon from my dreams shall I wa-ken to sor - row, To-
p
rall.
rall.
tempo.
heart long de - sponding with plea - sure fill - ing. Oh, sing, sing on
day give me rap-ture, I'll weep to - mor - row. Oh, sing, sing on
colla voce.
p
sweet - ly to cheer me, Sing of love, of love on - ly sing.
e'en to de - ceive me, Sing of love, of love on - ly sing.
mf
ff
marcato.

Published by Julius Berr.

tempo.
ad lib. imitatingly.
Sing, Sing, Ah! Ah! Ah! Ah!
pp
ad lib.
8va
portando.
Larghetto sostenuto.
Con forza e passione.
Ah! Ah! Ah! Ah! song - ster, pi - ty me!
ff
dim.
Why can I nev - er sing a song of rap - ture like
ff sempre.
1st.
thee?
2d.
thee.
p
rall.

Published by Jules Berr.

ORPHÉE AUX ENFERS.

QUADRILLE.

No. 1.
f
mf
f
p
CODA.
f
Fine.
p

D.C.
No. 2.
f
Fine.
ff
D.C. al fine.

No. 3.
CODA.
Fine.

No. 4.
f
Fine.
p
f
p
D.C.

Published by Jules Berr.

Finale.
mf
p
mf
To finish.
Fine.
ff
8va
Dal Segno.

Jerusalem the Golden.

A. EWING.

PIANO.
1. Je - ru - sa - lem the gold - en! With milk and hon - ey blest, Be - neath thy con - tem - pla - tion, Sink heart and voice op - prest. I know not, oh! I know not What joys a-wait us there; What ra - dian - cy of glo - ry, What bliss be - yond com - pare.
2. They stand, those halls of Zi - on, All ju - bi - lant with song, And bright with many an an - gel, And all the mar - tyr throng: There is the throne of Da - vid, And there, from toil re - leased, The shout of them that tri - umph, The song of them that feast.
3. And they, who with their Lead - er, Have conquer'd in the fight; For ev - er, and for ev - er, Are clad in robes of white. Oh, land that seest no sor - row! Oh, state that fear'st no strife! Oh, roy - al land of flow - ers! Oh, realm and home of life!
4. Oh, sweet and blessed coun - try! The home of God's e - lect! Oh, sweet and bless-ed coun - try, That ea - ger hearts ex - pect! Je - sus, in mer - cy bring us To that dear land of rest; Who art, with God the Fa - ther, And Spi - rit, ev - er blest.

Published by Jules Berr.

The Merriest Girl that's Out.

Words by CHARLES MERION. Arranged by CARLO NINASI.

Allegro spiritoso.
PIANO.
ff
cres.
1. With laugh - ter and good hu - mour, why, I pass my time a - way, So while I'm here I'll do my best to please you with my lay. Then
2. The gen - tle - men com - plain, and say, I'm such a dread - ful flirt, And if they will make love to me, their hearts I'm sure to hurt. I
3. The notes and pre - sents I receive would fill a bas - ket quite, While bou - quets rare, I do de - clare, are sent me ev' - ry night. The
4. To balls and par - ties I oft go, for danc - ing I ad - mire, And waltz - ing is a thing, I own, of which I nev - er tire. And
ff
mf
cres.
mf

 Published by Jules Berr.

come a - long, and join my song, and raise a mer - ry shout, To
real - ly can't help laugh - ing, when I hear them sigh a - bout, For
notes all speak of bro - ken hearts, some mean it, I've no doubt, I'm
should my part - ner squeeze my hand, I know what I'm a - bout, It
cres.
wel - come me, for I'm, you see, the mer - ri - est girl that's out.
sen - ti - ment, it don't suit me, I'm the mer - ri - est girl that's out.
sor - ry, yet I still re - main the mer - ri - est girl that's out.
pleas - es him, and don't hurt me, I'm the mer - ri - est girl that's out.
cres.
Chorus.
f
Now, then, young men, don't be me - lan - cho - ly; just see, like me,
ff

if you can't be jol - ly. If a - ny thing goes wrong with me, I
f
nev - er sulk, or pout; In fact, I am, and al - ways was, the
cres.
risoluto.
mer - ri - est girl that's out.
ff risoluto.
ff
cres.
ff

Published by Jules Berr.

COUSIN ET COUSINE.

SCHOTTISCH ELEGANTE.

JULES EGGHARD.

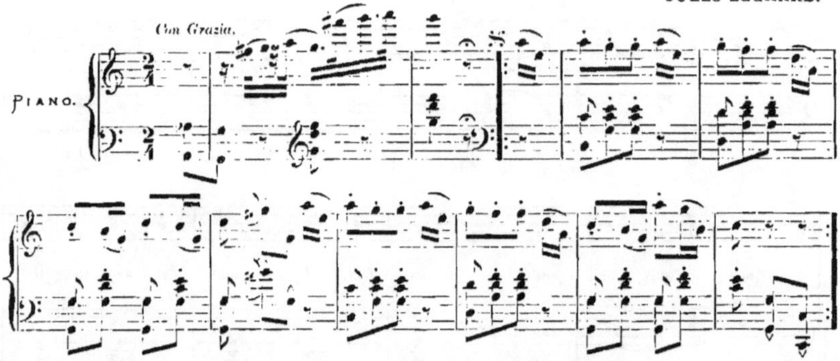
Con Grazia.
PIANO.

Con tutta Eleganza.
p
fz
f
dim.

dim.
fz
mf
dim.
p
cres.

Published by Jules Bers.

p
cres.
dim.
p
p
cres.
dim.
p
cres.
ff
mf
ff

Published by Jules Berr.

HOW FAIR ART THOU.

Wie schon bist Du.

H. WEIDT.

Moderato.
PIANO.
1. Oh, at thy feet, how hap - py, heart's in - most song I raise, Whilst eve's ma - jes - tic
2. Oh, at thy feet, how hap - py, thy beau - ty I ad - mire! A pi - teous smile glides
3. Oh, at thy feet, how hap - py, in si - lent pain to die! But ra - ther would I
gol-den light thro' the arch'd window plays. In mea - sure moves thy love - ly head, thy
o'er thy face, no pi - ty I de - sire. Well do I know thou play'st with me, yet
rise, my dear, and to thy bo - som fly, To press a thousand kiss - es on

Published by Jules Berr.

heart does lis - ten now, I lie be - fore thee sing-ing, I lie be-fore thee
rest - less am I now, And lie be - fore thee sing-ing, and lie be-fore thee
thine en-chant-ing brow; Then droop - ing down and dy - ing, yea, dy - ing, and still
cres - - - cen - - - do.
sing - ing, How fair, how fair, how fair art thou! How fair, how fair, how
sing - ing, How fair, how fair, how fair art thou! How fair, how fair, how
fair art thou!
fair art thou!
sf

Published by Jules Berr.

In the Starlight.

DUET.

Words by J. E. CARPENTER. Music by STEPHEN GLOVER.

Allegretto.
PIANO.
p
Ped.
mf
f
1. In the
2. In the

Published by Jules Berr.

star - light, in the star - light, let us wan - der gay and free; For there's
star - light, in the star - light, at the day - light's dew - y close. When the
p
decres.
noth - ing in the day - light half so dear to you and me; Like the
night - in - gale is sing - ing his last love - song to the rose, In the
dolce.
fai - ries in the sha - dow of the woods we'll steal a long, And our
calm, clear night of sum - mer, when the breez - es soft - ly play, From the
dolce.
p

 Published by Jules Berr.

dim.
rit.
sweet-est lay we'll war - ble, for the night was made for song; When
glit - ter of our dwell - ing we will gen - tly steal a - way. Where the
a tempo.
cres.
none are by to lis - ten, or to chide us in our glee, In the
sil - v'ry wa - ters mur - mur, by the mar - gin of the sea, In the
decres.
star - light, in the star - light, let us wan - der gay and free.
star - light, in the star - light, we will wan - der gay and free. In the
sf

Published by Jules Bern.

cres.
In the star-light, let us wan-der, In the
In the star-light, we will wan-der, In the
cres.
star-light, let us wan-der, In the
star-light, we will wan-der, In the
rit.
a tempo.
star - light, in the star - light, let us wan - der gay and free.
rit.
a tempo.
star - light, In the star - light, we will wan - der gay and free.
cres.
rit.
Ped.
Ped.
Ped.

J. G. MAXWELL
IMPORTER & MANUFACTURER OF
LADIES DRESS TRIMMINGS
S.E.Cor. 11th & Chestnut Sts
PHILAD.

On the Beach at Cape May.*

Words by E. N. SLOCUM.

Moderato.
PIANO.
f
p
1. On the Beach at Cape May, on an Au - gust day,
2. I ask'd her if she'd take a walk: she smiled, and said, "I will:" She

* Used by permission of Witzig & Co.

Published by Jules Berr

smo - king a ci-gar for to pass the time a-way, List'-ning to the waves as they
said it, too, with such a grace, me - thinks I hear her still, And as we walk'd a-long the beach to-
beat a - gainst the shore, I saw a love - ly form, I ne'er had seen be - fore. She
geth - er, arm in arm, I thought then if she'd marry me I'd keep her from all harm. I
wore a hand-some Gabrielle; her wa - ter - fall was high; Her eyes were large as sau - cers, her
felt just then all o - ver, I can - not tell you how; She turn'd on me her love-ly eyes, I
mf
nose turn'd to the sky: Oh, she was love - ly to be - hold! she
thought I'd faint, I vow; And smi - ling - ly she said to me, with

Published by Jules Berr.

stole my heart a - way, This fair, be-witching crea-ture that I met at gay Cape May.
such a pret - ty pout, "You fas - cin - a - ting crea-ture, does your mo-ther know you're out?"
Chorus.
On the beach at Cape May, on an Au-gust day, I saw this love-ly charmer who stole my heart a - way;
pp
Now I feel so bliss-ful, the hap - py moments glide, The day is quickly coming when she will be my bride.

3. We afterwards did bathing go, and now comes my mishap;
In venturing out beyond the rest, a wave struck her "ker"-slap;
It carried her unto the shore, and safely she did land,
My feet from under me did slip, I dove into the sand;
The people all began to laugh, as from the waves I rose,
Both eyes were shut and fill'd with sand, and bleeding was my nose;
I tried in vain to stand erect, but fell down all the more,
Until a gent compassion took, and led me to the shore. CHORUS.

4. Now all young gents,—you bucks, I mean,—remember what I say:
If you a sweetheart badly want, I recommend Cape May;
A wife to win and wear it is the place beyond a doubt;
But, first, before you go, be sure your mother knows you're out,
And if by chance you bathing go, don't venture out too far;
Just think of me, eyes fill'd with sand, enough to form a bar.
But try again, let people laugh, no matter what they say,
A jolly, laughing, merry set you'll find at gay Cape May. CHORUS.

Published by Jules Bert.

Dedicated to L. R. Lee.

SCHÜTZEN-MARSCH.

CARL FAUST.

PIANO.
ff
ff
p
p
fz

Published by Jules Berr.

8va
ff
8va
Imo.
2do.
p
p
fz

Published by Jules Berr

THE LEADING DEMOCRATIC PAPER OF PENNSYLVANIA.
A most desirable Advertising Medium,
"THE AGE,"
PUBLISHED IN THE AGE BUILDING,
Nos. 14 and 16 South Seventh Street, Philadelphia.
Terms of the Daily, $9.00 per Annum. Weekly, $2.00 per Annum.
WITH GREAT REDUCTION TO CLUBS.
All orders should be addressed to
WELSH & ROBB, Proprietors.
Fine.
TRIO.
p
p
f
p
f
ff
1mo.
2do.
1mo.
2do.
D. C. al Fine.

VOLL HUMOR.

POLKA.

INTRODUCTION. CARL FAUST.

Allegretto.
PIANO.
p
f
POLKA.
p

ff
1mo.
2do.
TRIO.
f
p
p
p

Published by Julius Bern.

LOUIS DREKA,
WEDDING, PARTY, VISITING AND BUSINESS
Card Engraving
Of the most approved style of the best material and workmanship.
1033 CHESTNUT St., Philada.
mf
1mo.
2do.
ff
Polka D.C. al ⊕
CODA.
f
p

Ohne Zügel und Bügel.

GALOP.

CARL FAUST.

INTRODUCTION.
GALOP.
PIANO.
f
p
fz
1mo.
2do.
tr
ff

Published by Jules Berr.

tr
tr
1mo.
fs
2do.
TRIO.
p

1mo.
2do.
ff
p
fz
CODA.

Ohne Zügel und Bügel.

Published by Jules Berr.

"Good Bye, Sweetheart, Good Bye."

JOHN L. HATTON.

Andante con Moto.
VOICE.
PIANO.
p
cres.
legato.
p
1. The bright stars fade, the morn is break - ing, The dew - drops pearl each bud . . . and leaf; And
2. The sun is up, the lark is soar - ing, Loud swells the song of chan - ti - cleer; The

Published by Jules Berr.

I from thee my leave am tak - ing, With bliss too brief, With
lev - 'ret bounds o'er earth's soft floor - ing, Yet I am here,
p
dim.
pp
ad lib.
bliss, ... with bliss . . . . too brief. How
Yet . . . . I . . . . am here. For
cres.
colla parte.
cres.
sinks my heart with fond a-larms, The tear is hid - ing
since night's gems from heaven did fade, And morn to flor - al
p
cres.
dim.
p
in mine eye, For time doth thrust me from thine arms; Good
lips doth hie, I could not leave thee, though I said, "Good
pp

Published by Jules Berr.

con moto.
bye, sweetheart, good bye, Good bye, sweetheart, good
bye, sweetheart, good bye. Good bye, sweetheart, good
molto cres.
bye; For time doth thrust me from thine arms; Good
bye;" I could not leave thee, though I said, "Good

LA CHATELAINE.

Allegro moderato. C. Faust.

Ped.
POLKA-MAZURKA.

 Published by Jules Berr.

TRIO.

Published by Jules Berr.

p
Polka-Mazurka D. S.
CODA.
ff
ff
ff

 Published by Jules Berr.

THE YOUNG RECRUIT.

A LA MILITAIRE. B. Richards.

Vivace.
ff
Ped.
* Ped.
*
Ped.
*
p piu lento.
a tempo.
ff
TEMA.
Tempo di Marcia.
f
Ped.
*
Ped.
*
Ped.
*
p
Ped.
*

Published by Jules Berr.

Ped.
Ped.
Ped.

Ped.
Ped.
Ped.
f

Ped.
8va

8va
Ped.
Ped.

Brillante.
Ped.
p

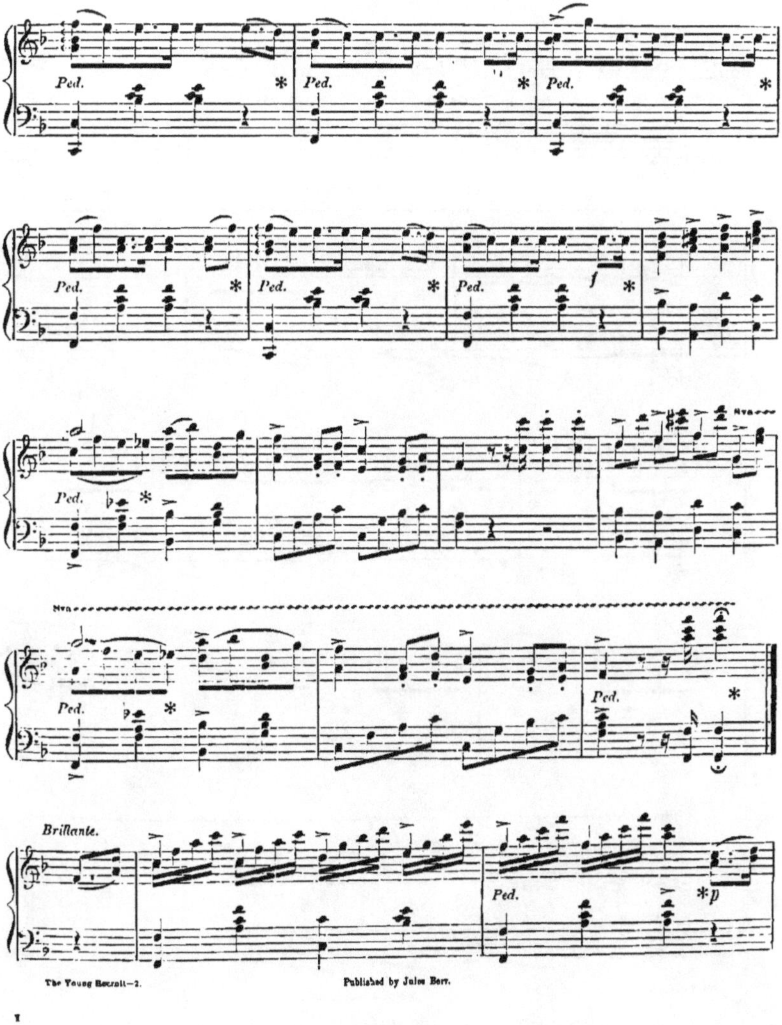

Ped.
8va
f
p
ff

Published by Jules Berr.

8va
Ped.
p
*
cres.
ff
f

Ped.
ff
8va
accell.
FINE

Published by Jules Berr.

"Five O'clock In The Morning."

BALLAD.

Written and Composed *By CLARIBEL.*

Moderato con espress.
PIANO.
p
1. The dew lay glitt'-ring o'er the grass, A mist lay o-ver the brook, At the ear-liest beam of the gold-en sun, The
2. And Bes-sie the milk-maid merri-ly sang, The meadows were fresh and fair, And the breeze of morn-ing kissed her brow, And
3. And o-ver the meadows the mow-ers came, And mer-ry their voi-ces rang, And one a-mong them wend-ed his way, To
cres.

 Published by Jules Berr.

swal-low her nest for - sook, The snow - y blooms of the
play'd with her nut - brown hair, But oft she turned, and
where the milk - maid sang, And as he lin - ger'd
p
haw - thorne tree Lay thick-ly the ground a - dorn - ing, The
looked a - round As if the si - lence scorn - ing, 'Twas
by her side, De - spite his com - rade's warn - ing, The
p
birds were sing - ing in ev' - ry bush, At five o' - clock in the
time for the mow - er to whet his scythe, At five o' - clock in the
old, old sto - ry was told a - gain, At five o' - clock in the

morn - ing, The birds were sing - ing in ev' - ry bush, At
morn - ing, 'Twas time for the mow - er to whet his scythe, At
morn - ing, The old, old sto - ry was told a - gain, At
five o' - clock in the morn - ing.
five o' - clock in the morn - ing.
five o' - clock in the morn - ing.
dim.
mf
tr

THE MOON BEHIND THE TREES.

G. T. WILSON.

Moderato.
PIANO.
1. In vis-ions bright I view a - gain my ear - ly childhood's scenes, For
p
fan - cy wafts me back to them, A - las! tho' but in dreams, . . . And

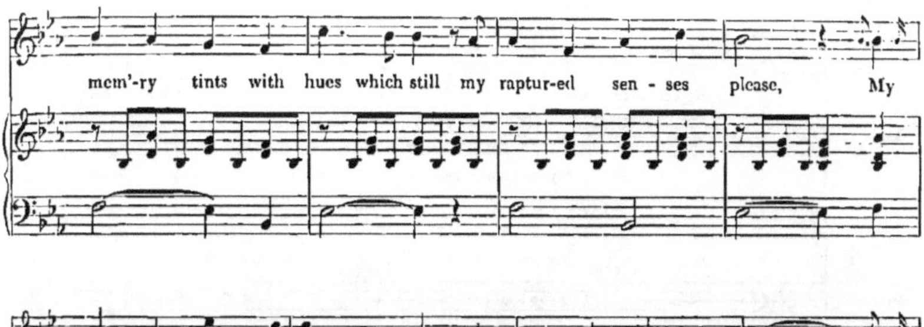
mem'-ry tints with hues which still my raptur-ed sen - ses please, My
cot - tage home, the streamlet, and the moon be - hind the trees, . . . My
cot - tage home, the streamlet, and the moon be-hind the trees.

CHORUS.

Tenor or Soprano.
My cot - tage home, My cot - tage home, and the moon be-hind the
Alto.
My cottage home, My cottage home, the moon be-hind the
Baritone.
My cottage home, My cottage home, and the moon be-hind the
Bass.
My cottage home, My cottage home, the moon be-hind the
PIANO.
trees, My cot - tage home, the streamlet, and the moon be - hind the trees. . . . .
trees, My cot - tage home, the streamlet, and the moon be - hind the trees. . . . .

BERG AUF, BERG AB.

UP AND DOWN.

GALOP.

CARL FAUST.

INTRODUCTION. *GALOP.*

PIANO.

Published by Jules Berr.

ff

TRIO.
ff
fz
p
f
p

fz
ff
1mo.
2do.
f
Galop D.C.
CODA.
fz

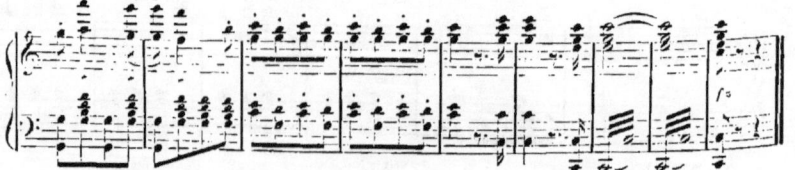

Published by Jules Berr.

THE BLACK-KEY POLKA MAZURKA.

A. HERZOG.

Tempo di Mazurka.

PIANO.
f
p stretto.
staccato.
f
p
pp
f
p

Published by Jules Berr.

3
p
f
pp
8va
p stretto.

Published by Jules Bort.

8va
f
staccato.
p
pp

Romance from Don Pasquale.

Arranged by THEODORE T. BARKER.

Larghetto cantabile.
Beau - teous and fair as au - gel bright,
PIANO.
p
On earth a pil - grim stray - ing, . . . Fresh as the li - ly's
robes of white, Sweet - ness at morn be - tray - - - - ing,

cres.
Bright eyes that speak while smi - ling Look, ev'-ry heart be -
gui-ling, ah! . . . Hair that can shame the dark-est night, Her
dolce.
smile seems some mag - ic spell; yes, seems some mag - ic spell.
f
poco più.
f
rall.

Published by Jules Berr.

Soul, spot-less, fair, and in - no - cent,
a tempo.
calando.
p
Her own heart still un-know - ing; Her mien, so mod-est and content, Its
sweet - ness on all be-stow - - ing, Pi - - ty the wretch - ed
show - - - ing, With love her breast o'er - flowing, ah! . . . . Form'd thus by heav'n to

Published by Jules Berr.

earth she's sent, In some blest heart to dwell, some heart . . to
Pressez.
dwell. Form'd thus by heav'n, to earth she's sent, In some fond heart to dwell, In some fond heart to
dwell. Form'd thus by heav'n, to earth she's sent, In some heart dwelling, a bless-
- - - - - - - - - - - - - - - ing, in some fond heart . . . . to dwell.

Published by Jules Bert.

Crispino e la Comare.

Opéra Bouffo des Frères RICCI.

FANTAISIE ÉLÉGANTE. *E. KETTERER.*

Andante.
PIANO.
p
mf
p
cres.
cres.

Published by Jules Berr.

mf

cres.
f
8va
p
cres.
f
pp
8va...
mf

f
cr. rall.
p
8va
f
p

p

8va..........
8va.......

8va.................
mf
cres.

ff
8va.....................

8va.
8va..........................
8va.........
f cres
cen
do.
ff
ff
ff

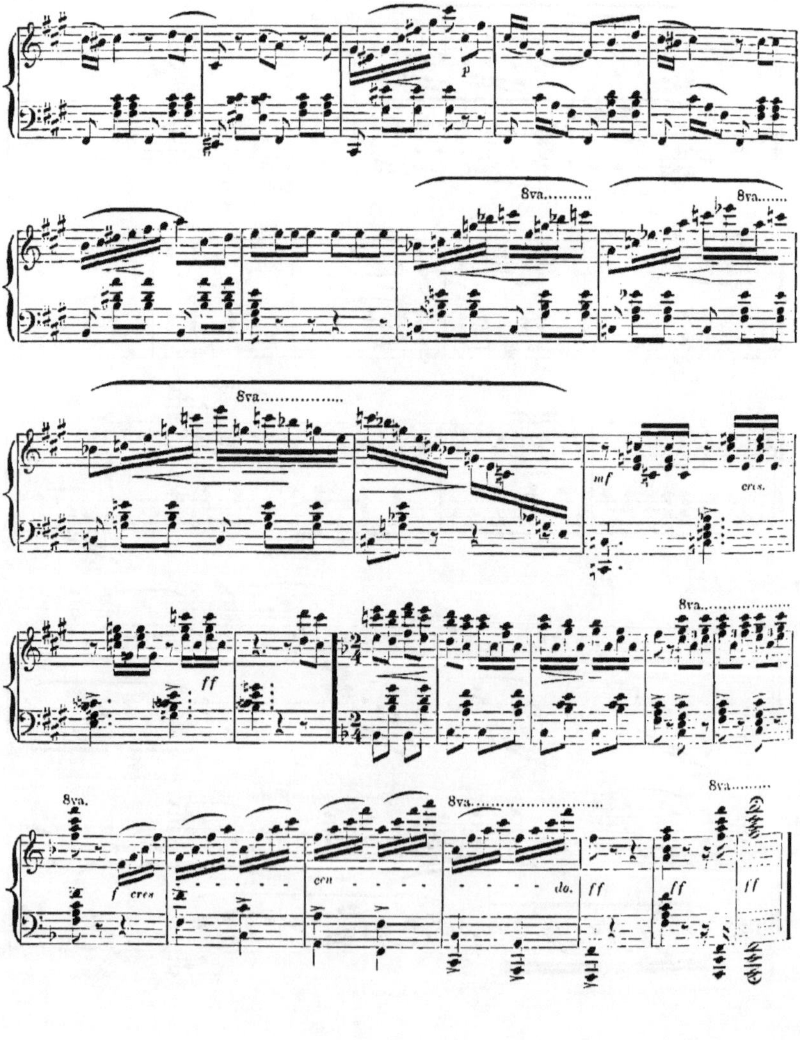

HOME SWEET HOME.

INTRODUCTION.
Moderato.

J. H. Slack.

ff
p
Cad. Veloce.
8va
Allo.
rit.
rall.

Published by Jules Berr.

TEMA.
Andante.
M. D.
con molto espress.
M. G.
Ped.

Published by Jules Berr.

VAR. I.

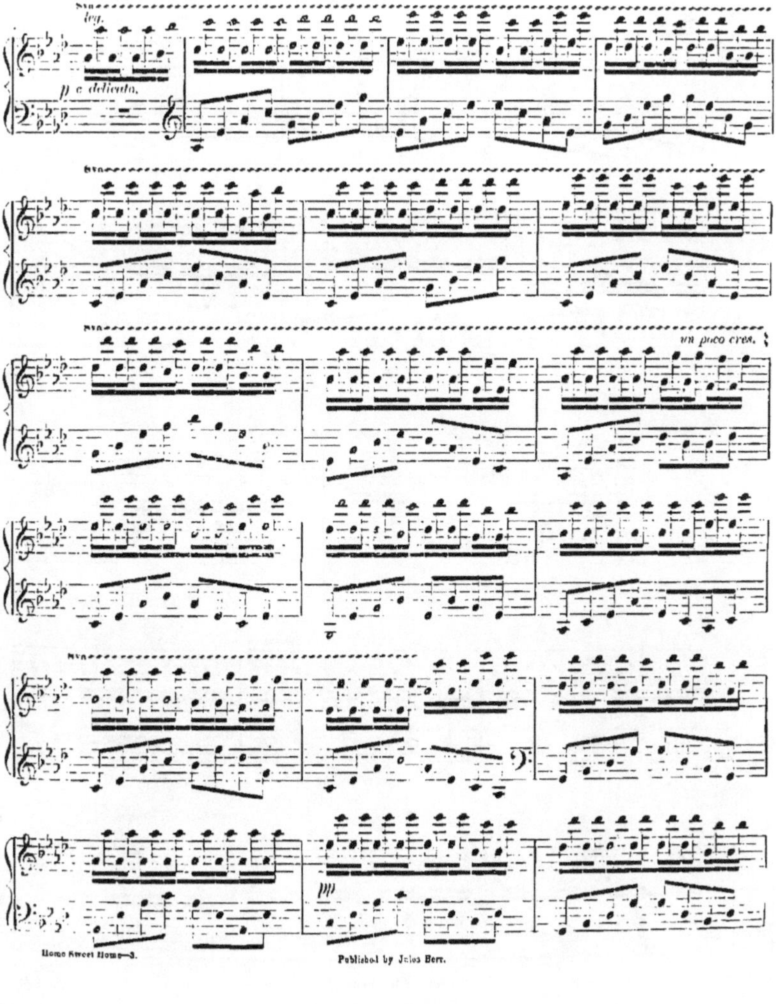
8va
leg.
p e delicato.
8va
8va
un poco cres.
8va
pp

8va
8va
f
f
ff
VAR. II.
Brillante.
f
La melodia ben marcato.

Published by Jules Bert.

FINALE.
Maestoso marziale.

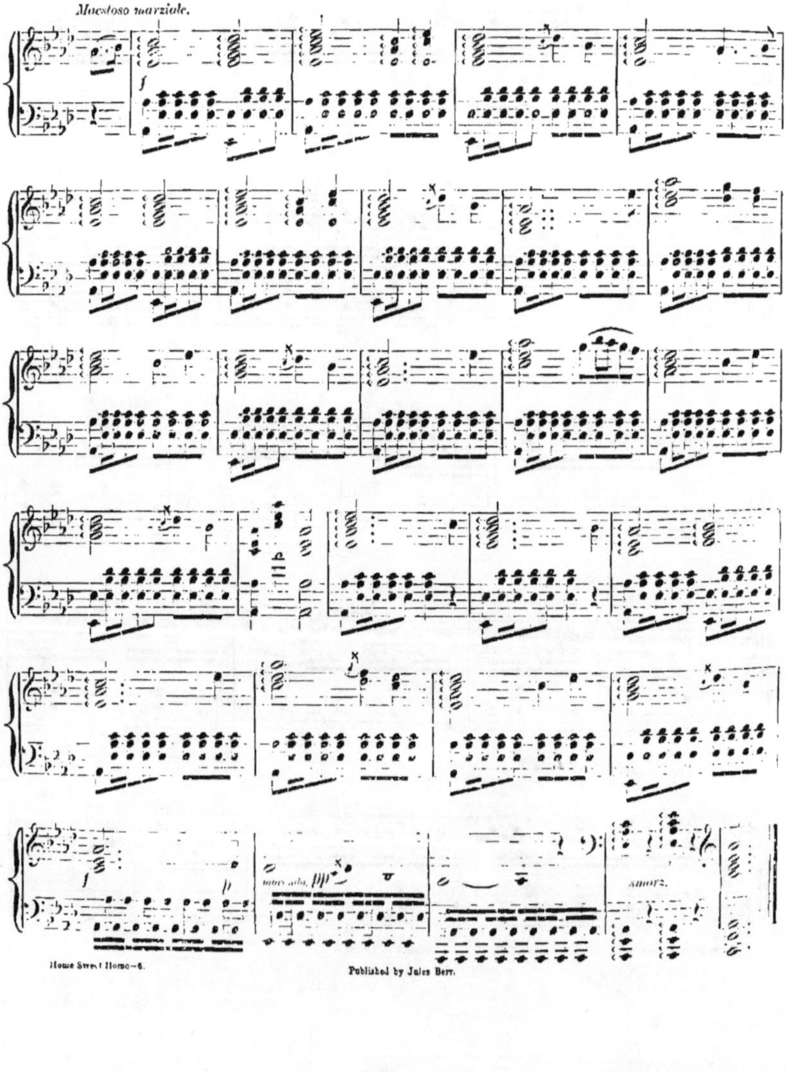
f
pp
smorz.

Published by Jules Berr.

MARCHE DES TAMBOURS.

MORCEAU MILITAIRE.

Sydney Smith.

Allegro marziale.
p
Ped.
sonore.
cresc.
f
cres - cen - do.
marcato e grandioso.
ff
Ped. * Ped. * Ped. * Ped. * Ped. *

Published by Jules Berr.

brillante.

Published by Jules Berr.

cantanto.
p
staccato.
dolce.
Ped.

Published by Jules Berr.

lourdement.
Ped.
leggiero.
8va

Published by Jules Bare.

8va
Ped.
Dal segno.
eguale
f

p grazioso e leggiero.
ff
8va
Ped.
ff
Ped.

Les Varietes Parisiennes.

L'INVITATION Valse.

8va
NO. 1.
Mouvement de Quadrille.
Salute to the right.
Salute to the left.
Right and left.
Cres......... cen......... do.
Mouvement de Valse.
Valse generale.

This figure to be played four times.

Published by Jules Berr.

L'ETOILE Polka.

Introduction.
NO. 2.
fp
fp
f
Mouvement de Quadrille.
p
Forward and
back two.
Chasse to the
right.
Right hand turn.
Forward and
back two.
Chasse to the right.
Right hand turn.
Mouvement de Polka.
L'Etoile.
fp
fp
f
fp
fp
f

This figure to be played four times.

Published by Jules Berr.

LE PRISONNIER Valse.

Introduction.
NO. 3.
Mouvement de Quadrille.
The gentleman invites successively the four ladies,
commencing with the one to the left.
Ladies hands round.
Mouvement de Valse.
Four couple form square in the centre.

This figure to be played four times.

Published by Jules Berr.

L'ALTERNANTE Mazurka.

Introduction.
Imo.
2do.
NO. 4.
ff
Mouvement de Quadrille.
Imo.
p
The gentleman
and lady
turn hands in
centre.
Moulinet.
by three.
Mouvement de Mazurka.
Left hand turn.
f Mazurka.
f
f

This figure to be played four times.

LA ROSACE Valse.

Introduction.
NO. 5.
f p
f p
f

Mouvement de Quadrille.
Forward two.
Salute and form line.
Forward and back Eight.
Ladies en Moulinet.
Mouvement de Valse.
La Rosace.
Coda.
Salut général.

This figure to be played four times.

Such figures of this Quadrille taken separately can be used in Cotillions.

Published by Jules Berr.

La Belle Hélène Galop.

Composed by OFFENBACH. Arranged by D. GODFREY.

INTRODUCTION.
PIANO.
ff
p
GALOP.
sf
p
cres.
cres.
ff

 Published by Jules Berr.

ff
ff
p
cres.
ff
cres.

TRIO.
f
ff
ff p
ff p
ff
ff
D. C.

Published by Jules Barr.

CODA.

p
cres - - - - cen - - -
- - do. ff
p
dim - in - u - cn - - - do.
p

ff
cres.
ff
ff

"Come Back to Erin."

SONG.

Words and Music by Claribel.

Moderato.
8va
PIANO.
Ped. * Ped. * Ped. * Ped. * Ped. * Ped. * Ped. *
1. Come back to E - rin, Ma - vour - neen, Ma-vour - neen,
2. O - ver the green sea, Ma - vour - neen, Ma-vour - neen,
3. Oh, may the an - gels, while wak - in' or sleep - in',
p
rit.
Come back, A-roon, to the land of thy birth, . . . Come with the sham-rocks and
Long shone the white sail that bore thee a - way, . . . Rid - ing the white waves that
Watch o'er my bird in the land far a - way, . . . And its my prayers will con-
col. voce.

Published by Jules Bem.

o

spring-time, Ma-vour-neen, And its Kil-lar-ney shall ring with our mirth.
fair sum-mer morn-in', Just like a May-flower a-float on the bay.
sign to their keep-in', Care o' my jew-el by night and by day.
f
Ped.
*
Ped.
*
p
Sure, when ye left us, our
Oh, but my heart sank when
When, by the fire-side, I
beau-ti-ful dar-ling, Lit-tle we thought of the lone win-ter days,
clouds came be-tween us, Like a grey cur-tain the rain fall-ing down,
watch the bright em-bers, Then all my heart flies a-way o'er the sea,

Published by Jules Berr.

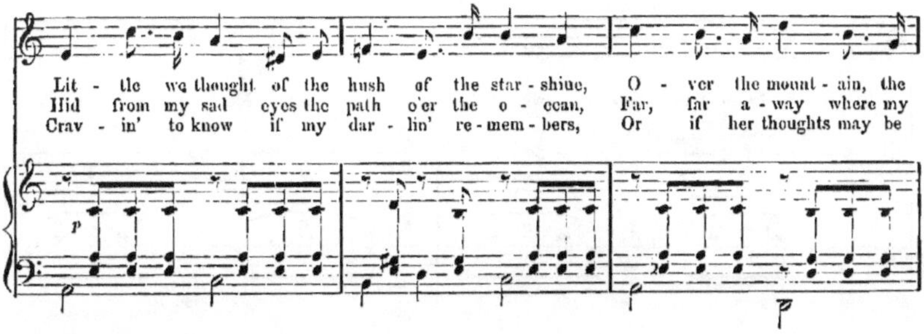
Lit - tle we thought of the hush of the star - shine, O - ver the mount - ain, the
Hid from my sad eyes the path o'er the o - cean, Far, far a - way where my
Crav - in' to know if my dar - lin' re - mem - bers, Or if her thoughts may be
p

Animato.
Bluffs and the Brays! Then come back to E - rin, Ma - vour - neen, Mavour - neen,
col - leen had flown. Then come back to E - rin, &c.
cross - in' to me. Then come back to E - rin, &c.
mf
Ped.

cres.
Come back to E - - - rin, Ma - vour - - neen, Ma - vour - neen,
molto cres.
And its Kil - lar - ney shall ring with our mirth.
8va
Ped.
*

Adrienne Polka Mazurka.

A. TALEXY.

PIANO.
sf
con forza.
1mo.
2do.

Published by Jules Berr.

dolce elegante.
grazioso.
sf
leggiero.
sf
sf
leggiero.

sf
brillante.
dim.
ff

Published by Jules Berr.

MAGGIE'S SECRET.

"OH, MANY A TIME I AM SAD AT HEART."

Words and Music by CLARIBEL.

Moderato.
PIANO.
p
rall.
a tempo.
1. Oh, ma - ny a time I am sad at heart, And I have - n't a word to say, And I keep from the lass - es and
2. Two sum - mers a - go, when a brave ship sail'd Far a - way to the gold - en West, Oh, . . . no - bo - dy knew that my

Published by Jules Bert.

lads a - part In the mea - dows a - mak - ing hay; . . . . . But
heart went too, For the se - cret I ne'er con - fess'd: . . . . A
Wil - lie will bring me the first wild rose, In my new sun - bon - net to
moth - er took leave of her boy that day, I could hear her sob . . . and
wear, ... And Rob - in will wait at the keep - er's gate, For he
cry, ... As I fol - low'd her back to her drear - y home, But . . .
fol - lows me ev - ery - where; . . . . But I tell them they need - n't come
nev - er a word said I; . . . . . . But I tell them, &c.

P

woo - ing to me, For my heart, my heart is o - ver the sea, But I
tell them they need - n't come woo - ing to me, For my heart, my heart is
o - ver the sea.
D.S.
Ending.

3. I sat by his mother one midsummer day,
And she look'd me through and through,
As she spoke of her lad who was far away,
For she guess'd that I loved him too;
She turn'd to me fondly and whisper'd low,
I was worthy her sailor boy,
My foolish tears they began to flow,
Though my heart beat high for joy.
|: So you see that they needn't come wooing to me,
For my heart, my heart is over the sea. :|

IM STRUDEL.

GALOP.

CARL FAUST.

INTRODUCTION.
PIANO.
ff
dim.
GALOP.
p
1mo.
2do.

Published by Jules Borr.

ff

TRIO.
f
p
p
mf

Published by Jules Berr.

1mo.
2do.
p
ff
ff
1mo.
2do.
Galop D.C.al ⊕
⊕ CODA.
mf
p
cres.
ff
fz

Blue Bird Polka Redowa.*

WEINGARTEN.

Tempo di Polka Redowa.
PIANO.
mf
ff
mf

* Used by permission of C. W. A. TRUMPLER.

Published by Jules Berr.

ff
mf
mf
mf

Published by Jules Berr.

TRIO.
mf

Dedicated to Miss Emma Akers.

BARBE BLEUE

(BLUE BEARD)

GALOP.

OFFENBACH. Arr. by THOS. A'BECKET, Jr.

INTRODUCTION.
ff
GALOP.
f
ff
p

 Published by Jules Berr.

ff
p
dolce.
p
1mo.
2do.
ff

1mo.
2do.
fz
fz
ff

Published by Jules Berr.

THE NAIAD'S BARCAROLLE.*

By E. MACK.

ff Ped.
p
cres.

* Used by permission of C. W. A. Trumpler

Published by Jules Berr.

Ped.
p

Published by Jules Berr.

Dedicated to Williams & Woodward.

FIRE AND FLAME.

(FEUER UND FLAMME.)

GALOP.

INTRODUCTION. Carl Faust. Op. 147

GALOP.

Published by Jules Berz.

TRIO.

1.
2.
Galop D. S. al ⊕
CODA.

Published by Jules Berr.

VICTORIA LANCERS.*

QUADRILLES.

Weingarten.

No. 1.

f
Fine.
f
p
f
D. C.

* Used by permission by C. W. A. Trumpler.

Published by Jules Berr.

No. 2.
ff
fs
Fine.
mf
D. C.

Published by Jules Berr.

No. 3.
mf
Fine.
mf
D. C.
No. 4.
f
Fine.
Grandioso.
f
Victoria Lancers—3.
Published by Jules Bert.

No. 5.

ff
p
p
ff
Fine.
f
mf
f
mf
f

Published by Jules Berr.

ff
f
mf
f
D. C.

 Published by Jules Berr.

LUCREZIA BORGIA.

(IL BRINDISI.)

DONIZETTI. Arr. by BURGMULLER.

RONDO.
PIANO.
Allegro.
p dolce.
cres.
p
cres.

Published by Jules Berr.

dim.
ff
p legg.
cres.
f
sf
p con delicatezza.

sf p
f
dim.
p
con affettuoso.
cres.
cres.
f
sf

p
sf p
f
f
dim.
D. C.

Published by Jules Berr.

8va
p legg.
8va
8va
8va
f
marcato.

cres. assai
8va
sf
sf
sf
sf
p con legg.
8va
cres.
f con fuoco
sf
sf
sf
sf

"Scenes that are Brightest."

OPERA OF MARITANA.

Music Composed by W. V. WALLACE.

Cantabile e con molta semplicità.
(Maritana.)
Voice.
Piano.
Ped.
pp
1. Scenes that are bright - - - est May charm . . . a - while . . . Hearts which are light - - est, And eyes . . . that smile; Yet
2. Words can - not scat - - - ter The thoughts . . we fear; . . . For, though they flat - - - ter, They mock . . . the ear. Hopes

Published by Jules Berr.

dim.
o'er them, a - bove us, Though . . na - ture beam, . . . With
will still de - ceive us With . . . tear - ful cost, . . . And
dolento.
none . . . . to love us, How sad . . . . they seem, . . . With
when . . . . they leave us, The heart . . . . is lost, . . . And
none . . . to love us, How sad . . . . they seem!
when . . . they leave us, The heart . . . . is lost.

MY FIRST WIFE'S DEAD.

BARBE BLEUE.

OFFENBACH. **Adapted by Dr. B.**

Allegro.
VOICE.
PIANO.
1. Oh, my first wife she is dead; But why should that trouble me, If I
2. Now my name you all do know, I told you what I am call'd, You will
know not how she died? Number two and num - ber
un - der-stand at once That I have one on - ly
three, Number four, too, all are gone. See me weep - ing, weeping
thought: 'Tis to fill her va - cant place, Fill the place of the

Published by Jules Berr.

for them all the same. And the fifth I loved so dear-ly; But last week, oh!
one I loved so dear. Be-tween us the thing is settled, That my sixth wife
p
tale of sor-row, Such is my as - ton - ish-ment, With no mo-tive
now is rea - dy, Yes, I know she soon will come! I do know, will
to dis-cov - er, Gath-er'd to the shades of her tomb, The three Fates have call'd her off!
you believe me? That al - rea - dy num-ber sev - en Vaguely oc - cu - pies my sight.

(with a terrible voice.)
Blue Beard is my name!
Blue Beard is my name!
f
Blue Beard, Blue Beard, Ah!
(very gayly.)
I am Blue Beard, I am he, wid - ow - er there nev - er was who
p

Published by Jules Berr.

is so gay as I, Blue Beard, wid - ow - er ne'er was so gay as
I, ah!
There was nev - er yet a wid - ow - er so gay as I, I am Blue
Beard. Blue Beard, Blue Beard is my name, oh! Blue Beard is my

name, Blue Beard is my name.
Blue Beard, Blue Beard is my name, oh! Blue Beard is my
name, Blue Beard, Blue Beard, Blue Beard, Blue Beard!
1mo.
2do.
Now my

Les Adieux.

(NOCTURNE.)

P. HORRO.

Andantino Cantabile.
PIANO.
pp
Ped.
poco cres.
dim.
cres.

Published by Jules Bert.

8va
Ped.
p
cres.
f
dim.
a tempo
poco rall.

Ped.
8va.
pp
Ped. dim.
rall. perdendosi.

Published by Jules Berr.

U

FRA DIAVOLO.

SYDNEY SMITH.

PRIERE. *Andante religioso.*

CANTANDO.
PIANO.
p
Con moto espress.
Ped. * Ped. *
dolce con tenerezza.
8va
p
delicato.

Published by Jules Berr.

grazioso.
Ped.
Ped.
rit.
piu mosso.
f
f
BARCAROLLE.
ff
ff ff
Allegretto.
Ped.
8va
Ped.
Ped.
Ped.
Ped.
Ped. Ped.
Ped. Ped.
Ped.
ff
ff
tremolo
p

Published by Jules Bett.

VARIATION.
Molto vivace e brillant.
8va
Ped.

8va
Ped.
f
grazioso.
p
dim.
Ped. dim.
cantabile con espress.

8va
p
Ped.
piu animato.
8va
ff
ff
8va
dim.
p
Ped.
p
leg.

cres.
con spirito.
ff Ped.
Ped.
f
p
ff
8va

Published by Jules Berr.

8va
Ped.
brillant

Valse des Roses.

E. KETTERER.

Alle. Brilliante.
cres.
p
dim.
8va
f

Published by Jules Berr.

8va
f
p
f
dim.
f
dim.
8va
f
p cres.
Ped.
Ped.
p cres.
dim.
f dim.

Published by Jules Berr.

dim.
p
cres.
Ped.
f
legg.

Published by Jules Borr,

1ma.
2do.
legg.
p
cres.
8va
mf
f
ff
dim.
a tempo.

Published by Jules Berr.

dim.
a tempo.
f
p
cres.
8va
p

p
p
rall.
dim.
a tempo.
f
Ped.
8va
ff

Cujus Animam.

De l'Opera STABAT MATER.

W. KUHE.

Allegretto maestoso.
PIANO.
f
8va
con fuoco.
ff
Ped.
semp. ff
e accel.
pausa.
ma sonore.
dim.

f
pomposo.
molto.
rf
8va......
semp. ff
Ped.
8va....
8va....
8va...
8va....
8va....
Ped.
semp. ff
c martell.
Ped.
string.
Ped.

Published by Jules Berr.

Armonioso e dol. cantando.
rf
assai.
pp
Ped.
8va
brillant.
f

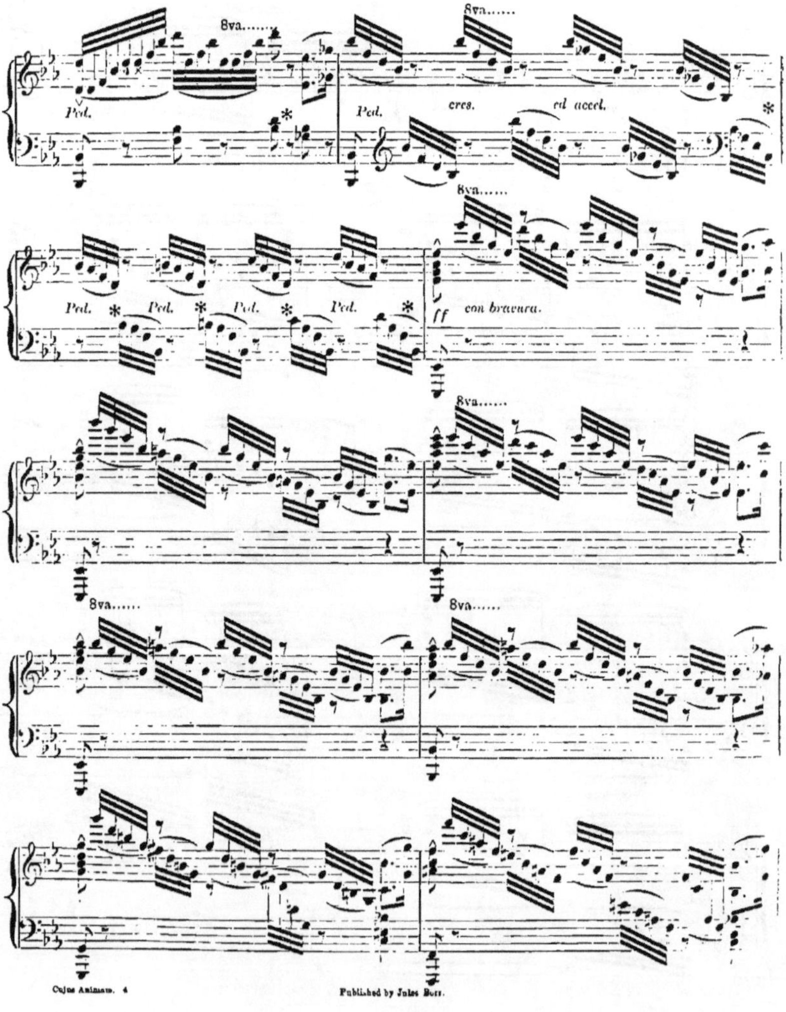
8va......
Ped.
cres.
ed accel.
ff
con bravura.

leg.
poco
a
poco.
cres.
accel.
f
8va.
loco
ff con bravura.
dim.

con grazia.
p
dim.
8va
loco
sempre. p
poco rall.
a tempo.
più vivo.
8va
loco
cres.
f
Presto.
8va
ff martellato.
8va.
prestissimo
8va.
con tutta la forza.
Ped.

La Favorite.

MORCEAU DE CONCERT.

J. Ascher.

Allegro moderato.
PIANO.
ff
mf
cres.
8va
loco.
poco - - a - - poco -

Published by Jules Berr.

8va
dim.
mf
p
8va
dim.
morendo.
rallent.
loco.
pp
Andante.
dolce.
p
p
poco rit.
rit.

p
cres.
8va
una corda.
loco.
dim. e rall.
p
pp
loco.
rit.
a tempo.
con amore.
leggiero.
poco rall.
cres.
f
ff
rit.

 Published by Jules Berr.

a tempo.
ff
mf
f
8va
f=
mf
loco.
8va
loco.
8va
p
f
p
f
dim.
8va
molto riten.
markato il canto.
pp una corda.
loco.
8va
loco.
p sempre.
8va
loco.
8va
loco.
molto riten.
pp a tempo.
8va

 Published by Jules Borr.

8va
loco.
mf
f
fz
rallent.
pp molto legato.
una corda.
p
cres
cen - - - do.
mf p
pp
dim.
rit.
dim.
pp molto riten. perdendosi.
Fine.

Published by Jules Berr.

Immortellen Waltz.

J. GUNG'L.

SECONDO.

No. 1.
p
Ped.
*
pp
cres.
f
p
cres.
f
p

Published by Jules Barr.

Immortellen Waltz.

J. GUNG'L.

PRIMO.

No. 1.
p
Ped.
cres.
pp
f
8va

Published by Jules Barr.

SECONDO.

No. 2.
Ped.
mf
f
p
1me.
2de.

PRIMO.

No. 2.

8va
p
Ped.
Ped.
Ped.

8va
Ped.
Ped.
cres.
f
Ped.
Ped.

1mo.
2do.
8va
p
p
Ped.

8va
Ped.
f
Ped.
Ped.
dim.

8va
1mo.
2do.
p
Ped.
Ped.
Ped.

SECONDO.

No. 3.
No. 4.
1mo.
2do.
decresc.

Published by Jules Berr.

PRIMO.

8va
No. 3.
Ped.
1mo.
2do.
ff
No. 4.
p dolce.

SECONDO.

f
Ped.
Ped.
p

No. 5.
p
Ped.
Ped.

Ped.
Ped.

ff
Ped.
Ped.
Ped.
Ped.

ff
Ped.
Ped.
Ped.
Ped.
Ped.

PRIMO.

No. 5.
8va
Ped.
p
f
ff

Published by Jules Bert.

DEDICATED TO MRS. A. C. VAN BEIL.

KÜNSTLER LEBEN.

ARTIST'S LIFE.

JOHANN STRAUSS.

WALTZ.
1.
p
pp
1mo.
2do.
f
1mo.
2do.
last time.

Published by Jules Berr.

2.
p
p
cres.
pp
cres.
f
pp
f
p
p
pp
pp
1mo.
2do.
Last time.

Published by Jules Berr.

3.
4.
Last time.

1mo.
2do.
5.
1mo.
2do.
1mo.
2do.

Published by Jules Berr.

Dedicated to Miss Clara V. Pote.

SANGER'S LUST MARCH.

PIANO.

Published by Jules Berr.

tr
mf
f
1ma.
2da.
Fine.
f p sf
p
sf
p

1ma.
cres.
sf
2da.
p
f
8va
8va
loco.
1ma.
2da.
D.C.

www.ingramcontent.com/pod-product-compliance
Lightning Source LLC
Chambersburg PA
CBHW030832270326
41928CB00007B/1008
* 9 7 8 3 7 4 4 7 9 2 9 9 8 *